FINISHING LINE PRESS
www.finishinglinepress.com

RABBIT RABBIT

poems by

Deb Jannerson

Finishing Line Press
Georgetown, Kentucky

RABBIT RABBIT

ACKNOWLEDGMENTS

The author wishes to thank her friend and colleague, Jessica Morey-Collins.

Editor: Christen Kincaid

Cover Art: Catherine Eyde

Author Photo: Steve Hammond

Cover Design: Elizabeth Maines

Printed in the USA on acid-free paper.
Order online: www.finishinglinepress.com
                         also available on amazon.com

Author inquiries and mail orders:
Finishing Line Press
P. O. Box 1626
Georgetown, Kentucky 40324
U. S. A.

Table of Contents

For anyone strong enough to break the cycle

rabbit rabbit

it's a dirty secret,
a false-bottomed drawer for a logical type.

it's reassurance: i did all i could,
now must heed the mercy of the
mystical, lawless, likely null fates

or else,
a missed step, a receptacle for
my hazy, dissatisfied blame.

something i cannot believe in,
but who can fully know?

a concession to superstition,
to the ropes i slipped from my brain,
the cracks which i sacrifice for skipping,
the wood untouched by my impotent fists.

fingerprint

It's a bruise, I said.
I felt her stiffen,
remembering
the book. A hardback novel,
though the grim humorist in me
imagined a Bible.
Let me see shoved back open
my door, greasy fingerprints
rubbing the cloud
below my hairline,
begging one last
wish.
A sharp chuckle, relief, delight:
No! It's just dirt.
She rubbed harder,
erasing,
evidence fading like a
dream.

one who games

she sleeps feet away,
red hair like seaweed
falling out of her cocoon, safe
in the thick dark of my
heartbreak.

i spin myself in water of
cyan pixels, barracudas i can
obliterate with another hour of
practice and luck.

imagine if she woke up.

it could be so embarrassing,
solo lights on my face,
respectability unpeeled
as i work myself toward the hypnotic oblivion
she harbors in her own
unplugged mind.

the mother

you cannot control the lips in my bed,
the rhythmic thorns at my keys,
the provocation of my figure
however you figure,
the rainbow vying from my scarred arms.

now, you can only
screech to the air and hope for echoes,
desperate sounds spitting through electricity,
denying, rewriting
lashed tongue from afar.

i capture the poison for the law
and castrate it for my health,
and lo:
like a melted witch or disappearing ink,
it dies.

edible

brownie oil takes ninety minutes to hit the blood,
one-point-five hours of christmas morning
jitters and public service
flashbacks, until the air proceeds to pulse with
profundity.

thoughts birth quickly as
gremlins, ancestors dying immediate and beautiful
deaths, each generation remembering less as it
grows, an infancy in
reverse.

tastes in tidal waves,
i skate on the world with
young eyes restored, squelching
distractions for days to
come.

i am connected, brilliant, exhaling color
as muddy crumbs like ugly duckling
sparkles sprinkle
to the wavy ground.

survivor

once,
i was only afraid
they would know

the long looks, fluttery chest
deep-buried photos PG yet pornographic
with my desire

the high-end needles, minute math games
the rapid distance in their eyes
registering defect

the hands, intrusion
my baffling, desperate body a
fractured shell

the talked-down knives, multiplied bottles
my father's fist clacking the soft spot
beneath my chin.

now,
i strive toward power but
pray to an absent god

that the strife
does not glow from a
flawed, hopeless core.

shy

i turn myself inside out in an
effort to put my best coat
forward, but my slippery
skin congeals, curled edges shying
away in terror as the tiny
tinny voice in my cotton-filled
chest pleads for a backwards
clock, a real-life standard time of poppy
forgetfulness, to swath my
epidermis in plainclothes camouflage
or else
to replay the inversion with more
gusto, pustules popping in polarizing
spectacle, so i may be argued but never
forgotten.

poorly

i have hunched in my bare
dwelling, hypoglycemic
trembling, sunken fox
eyes on the minute, as
i await the motion of
the sketchy, impassive
national god.

i have spewed the sparse
contents of my mannequin
figure beside a night of
labor, short-circuiting
shell in an earthquake,
begging for a
pharmacy counter.

i have watched the sanitized
digits of fortune blink, one
two three four,
absorbing the weight of
my crackling, deformed spine and
relieving the
funny bone famish.

but I'll never have the
grace to not worry
again.

agoraphobic haiku

bald vulnerable
wrapped in my home like blankets
i keep the hands out

the scale

the rainbow cartoon hosts bloody fangs
twee and grotesque hands clasped
on a fine-weighted scale
like
the girl with the curl or
christmasland's hook-teeth
like
warm cake and cool cream or
thunder and kisses
like
maddening episodals or
spherical yin-yangs
like
hel's grand self-torment or
you and i

untitled

day is a fair friend
but night is a home
leave the moon on for me, love
i still wish to roam

when you write erotica

people tend to assume the
tales with which you regale anonymous masturbators are
flashbacks or fantasies, and
early on this may be
true.

but when your spring chicken-choking status has
expired, the pursuit of a pulsating phrase becomes
clinical, and, to the careless,
formulaic, a ten-page geometry proof more
fated than florid, and decidedly
unsexy.

as remedy, i
lean through the red leather and scrim curtains toward
absurdity, toward bubbling aliens with blobs of bodies and
inappropriate analogies to foodstuffs, with
smoke alarm caterwauling and
snail-trail mucus making sticky work of
sheets.

but as this is disrespect or disillusionment
to tell, it remains merely shown, and i
shorthand a soundbite:
you gotta keep things interesting somehow.

exhaust

days without dozing were
tallied as trophies, though at
my hot weathered core i knew
myself powerless

the warm, drenched blanket
found me minus effort
classroom, car, business
left me pink as washed blood

the body's original sin
simplest betrayal, imprinted in
seconds of birth, sawed lumberyard
buries my self-pinching to still

chalky white pills, beverage thin
with a lack of distractions
hold no rousing candle

until i succumb

armchair

in cautious textbooks, pate-dry, or campuses bleeding passion
we absorb atrocities to the will and flesh
bemoaning the old days of shackles and spectacle
safely inferior by a long line of four-digit numbers

we read, cry mildly, recite wacky facts
the unveil, the gold coins, the scale-weighted shame
expressionless freak show smooth of human/humaneness
ripe for cynicism and isaac asimov

out of the airlocked cube, pale eyes own the terrain
debate tags, guffaw choices of specified specimens
thinking ourselves generous for the good one exceptions
quick to forget we don't write our own history

this horror tinge may linger long as people are alive
not cruelty of the singular, but groupthink of the hive

grow

it's quite a thing,
that *pizza* has two Zs in a row when so
few mutterings in the U.S.
vernacular have any

like the '90s would-be trenders
the *Skool 2 Skool* and *Awesome Binder* lot
it seems misleading, misteaching
impractical

an extravagant staple in a
tamped-down blooming life, it feeds
its own appeal, harmless mischief as
acceptable camouflage

for the fingers, the blasphemers
mind floating from fences, all that they
cross
now unfit to be seen

the growers are turned from
for the allure of fond chuckling
recalling that poster on
jello and kids' minds

excuse

a little brother is
a classic scapegoat
a sitcom staple

It Was Him
they say.
the lamp
the mess
the idea

an innocent cloak
from the parents
grows hunchbacked into
a dubious dark charm
for the parents

the tears
the limp
the rug burn
It Was Him
i said.

they stopped asking

the last word

our portable toy hangs in
plain sight, a plane flourish
floating, flaming strength in
boundaries, evolved child cookie thrill.

more subversive still, a supposed
symbol of quiet dominance, of
mannish assumption not to be
found under your shell.

it is privy to color debates,
impassioned as innocence, before
going gory past our front door,
dual power plug self-charging.

together, we taste test restraint, the
sparks hidden in the murky soup of
our unconscious, extinguishers pointed
in detailed control.

we have fractures from kid larks, from
trauma and violence, and defense in this
modest plaid scrap we can
tie.

an agoraphobe's well-being is

like a tower of blocks or cards
stacked, observed, glued in phases like a
ziggurat, awaiting a hard enough shake for
the crack and imbalance, the
skill and intent of its builder
null

like a pitch opaque sticky forest
collapsing, rotating, in time with an
arrhythmic heart, disorienting a
nightmarish wonderland, the
right to see one's enemies
denied

like a dark resigned pragmatism
cobbled together of
bootlegs, deliveries, humiliating favors and
days lined like plath's boxes
small goodies to rival a void of
trust

like a medically induced slept away day
writhing fitfully as an
ancient fever, walls in a
firm cube, cloistered
from the faceless, dissatisfied yellers but not the
mind

self check

you know my
night habits, my
clouded eyes after the attack, my
brand of sausage.

like most the corner machines'
patrons, i seek to avoid such
personal flourishes, such
reverse-velvet small talk, such
accidental intimacies.

the lights put us on
a stage of tedium, on
a hovering bubble, on
the same plain.

how long until they
replace you, too, and i
don't have to lend you a
pantry in my mind?

i demur to the end aisle,
sacrificing convenience and a
coolly rational metal exchange to
hide.

the seed

i.
the kindergarten upstart asked
why he couldn't marry his friend
if females were so slight and
foolish for apples

because that's terrible
she said, and the
toddler's eyes frosted as he
disappeared into his reshaping mind

the older needed more, and so:
it takes over their lives
and out spilled the anecdotes

she once knew someone
saw someone
heard of someone
unashamed

instead of starving or infecting wounds
those miscreants grew robust and stretched for
contentment, that black magic
simply to gall her

ii.
improbably, the older rose and
wore her battered self on her screen
the jailer's failure
a non-fatal acid

someone help
she then spat to the faceless millions
our daughter is dangerous
maul her down
gnaw her up
cough her out
until those eyelids get lowered

hidden within was the
seed of her wrath and
every serpent on medusa's head:
she's probably happy

the child's art was not martyrdom
scars not a technicolor dreamcoat
healing, that black magic
simply to taunt her

it takes over their lives
she said
and now i recognize the
jealous flaw in the lens

visit

smoke-addled beforehand
i try to explain

minus linus, shamed for ty
humor has snuggled into my collarbone

yet sharp lips and loose hips evaporate
in the face of your haze's murky form

the room-sized elephant
is a commanding element

i tie myself in squares

storm

when working at an outdoor café
Camera or Lightning
is a common game

equating the frivolous and cataclysmic
is a stiff drink, a dark whistle
an ignorant hug

the gutters, maps, power-outs
are dust mites for pawing
eyes turned from memories of ruins and roofs

we stare at our timelines
nervous and small
wondering which shoe was which

sexy barbie rapunzel

you yell
blissfully unbound from the
what-do-they-think of
female education.

your dime-dozen hoots
poke me into the ground like
a nail with
phantom pounds from conviction of the
skeleton key in your pants.

another tiny weight between my shoulder
blades, a further contortion in
my wavy spine
a brother scar of night terrors and
feeble days without sun.

you cast me as plaster
casted as plastic
blank word-bubble princess for
your pleasure, your status
your story.

defenders will point to an
ignorant innocence
the luck of the gender
a sickness of social grace
a mistake.

yet here we are
explaining with a million lips
bleeding rage
exhaling truth
and you have no excuse.

football

i only knew
which days
by the number of
bottles.

nightmare bracelet

as a towheaded child star
i fled hell at dusk
each sun-spin an unwelcome interlude from
the mottled, shine-drenched wanderings of my mind

at my actual-size rebirth
i pried each sticky frog finger
from my pressure points and
quivered the swamp from my boots

it made a fineprinted trade

for now i return
an inverted persephone
former straw hut safe haven turned
nightmarish

locked in my mind by
my hapless husk body
yelps and convulsions melt as my
lover pulls me toward shore

my wrist rolls attempt to
further bleach the yin-yang
old magic, kid whimsy
a nod to the unknown

i am casually held
by mama cat comfort
from what i escaped and from
what i still flee

Deb Jannerson is a New Orleans-based poet and author of bildungsroman fiction, queer romance, and children's horror and sci-fi. She has stories in *Best Lesbian Erotica 2015* and the forthcoming collection *My Gay New Orleans*. Her New Adult novella, *Further*, was a finalist in the 2014 William Faulkner—William Wisdom Competition. Her work has appeared in many magazines, including *Bitch*, *Nola Live,* and *Women's Review of Books*.

Learn more at deborahjannerson.com and facebook.com/ DebJannersonWrites.